PYRAMID OF BONE

Volume 8
THE CALLALOO POETRY SERIES
Charles H. Rowell, Series Editor

PYRAMID OF BONE

Thylias Moss

University Press of Virginia
Charlottesville

THE UNIVERSITY PRESS OF VIRGINIA
Copyright © 1989 by the Rector and Visitors
of the University of Virginia

First published 1989

A number of poems in this volume originally ap-
peared in the following periodicals and are re-
printed by permission—*Callaloo:* "One for All
Newborns," "Lesson from a Mirror," "A Reconsi-
deration of the Blackbird," "To Eliminate Vague-
ness," "*Timex* Remembered," "*The Road to Todos
Santos* Is Closed"; *Indiana Review:* "Back to the
Hyena," "The Owl in Daytime," "The Undertak-
er's Daughter Makes Bread," "The Undertaker's
Daughter Feels Neglect," "Doubts during Catas-
trophe"; *The Gamut:* "Good Amnesia"; *Graham
House Review:* "Landscape with Saxophonist."

Special thanks to the Artist's Foundation of
Massachusetts and to the Kenan Charitable Trust

Library of Congress Cataloging-in-Publication Data

Moss, Thylias.
    Pyramid of bone / Thylias Moss.
        p.   cm. —(The Callaloo poetry series ; v. 8)
    ISBN 0-8139-1202-4 : $8.95
    I. Title.   II. Series.
PS3563.08856P9 1989
811′.54—dc19   88-25855
                                                    CIP

Printed in the United States of America

*For my mother who made it to the dean's list
of preferred housekeepers; she is a maid of honor.
This book is for her and in memory of her
nephew Lawrence.*

CONTENTS

PYRAMID OF BONE

ONE FOR ALL NEWBORNS

They kick and flail like crabs on their backs.
Parents outside the nursery window do not believe
they might raise assassins or thieves, at the very worst
a poet or obscure jazz musician whose politics
spill loudly from his horn.
Everything about it was wonderful, the method
of conception, the gestation, the womb opening
in perfect analogy to the mind's expansion.
Then the dark succession of constricting years,
mother competing with daughter for beauty and losing,
varicose veins and hot water bottles, joy boiled away,
the arrival of knowledge that eyes are birds with clipped wings,
the sun at a 30° angle and unable to go higher, parents
who cannot push anymore, who stay by the window
looking for signs of spring
and the less familiar gait of grown progeny.
I am now at the age where I must begin to pay
for the way I treated my mother. My daughter is just like me.
The long trip home is further delayed, my presence
keeps the plane on the ground. If I get off, it will fly.
The propeller is a cross spinning like a buzz saw
about to cut through me. I am haunted and my mother is not
    dead.
The miracle was not birth but that I lived despite my crimes.
I treated God badly also; he is another parent
watching his kids through a window, eager to be proud
of his creation, looking for signs of spring.

THE WRECKAGE ON THE WALL OF EGGS

I cried over Humpty-Dumpty.
My indulgent parents permitted mock funerals
after every breakfast. The wall is what upset me,
Humpty's segregation which I doubt he chose.
The King's obligatory visit to the site of disaster.
I cried eggs then double dutched through shells.
One summer I logged a hundred miles in the driveway.
I was after the King's men and had no hope of catching them
since I lived on the wall. Total unobstructed vision
and I loathed it. On both sides were hundreds of girls
perfect for the part of Heidi.
My jump rope flew like long braids I didn't have.
The granite street was a long tombstone for my grandfathers
and their fathers. Following it would not lead to Dörfli
in the Alps. The easiest thing was to keep looking east and west
and hating girls who couldn't control ancestry.
On the wall, all we ever want is easiness.
Egg shells keep turning up on the path, the humpty-dumpties
spill from me and die like so many babies mercy-killed
out of slavery.
My life on the wall is anything but easy.
I want to but can't hate Heidi well.
I can't maintain tragic responses to breaking eggs.
When I look down at the wreckage on the wall of eggs that
came out of me, I see that what's inside is as white and
gold as Heidi.

LESSONS FROM A MIRROR

Snow White was nude at her wedding, she's so white
the gown seemed to disappear when she put it on.

Put me beside her and the proximity is good
for a study of chiaroscuro, not much else.

Her name aggravates me most, as if I need to be told
what's white and what isn't.

Judging strictly by appearance there's a future for me
forever at her heels, a shadow's constant worship.

Is it fair for me to live that way, unable
to get off the ground?

Turning the tables isn't fair unless they keep turning.
Then there's the danger of Russian roulette

and my disadvantage: nothing falls from the sky
to name me.

I am the empty space where the tooth was, that my tongue
rushes to fill because I can't stand vacancies.

And it's not enough. The penis just fills another
gap. And it's not enough.

When you look at me,
know that more than white is missing.

DEVELOPMENT OF AN ADULT NIGHTMARE

It starts when gathering mynas
create the darkness.

They broadcast
what I didn't mean to say aloud.

They are sassy and talk back
every bit the disobedient child I was.

What they say shouldn't bother me
since I've heard it before.

But they don't let me forget anything
no matter how insincere the promise.

The mynas are never more than a foot away
within the range where my myopia has no effect.

There's nothing I can do about them
always having the last word.

The rock path to my house is the only trace
of a huge animal buried up to the teeth.

It is being punished
for feeding mynas.

They can keep a secret
only if I keep it first.

They have no flair for art
confusing the white lies with the black.

I must be the initiator of praise.
It is also my fault if there is no politeness.

I learn to say what I want to hear.
They learn not to want anything.

In frustration I curse them.
They curse themselves without emotion.

As a Christian
I'm supposed to want to be this humble.

Do they believe everything or nothing?
They ask me to tell them.

Yesterday I would have fought against segregation.
Yesterday I would have fought for freedom of speech.

Now here I am freeing the world of mynas.
Here I am stuffing them down the throat

of an animal already aware of its limitations.
Who has the right to hate the myna, someone like me

who cannot understand their ways
or the one who has to be a myna?

Even though they're gone,
Even though my thoughts are mine alone now,

I think of mynas.

BACK TO THE HYENA

I should go back because the spotted animal
can go for days without drinking
and I've needed Bacardi to give fantasized pirates

a liquid medium in which to pilot their ships
to my bedroom. They're invited
only because they are given to womanizing.

Long nights at sea in a rocking vessel
conjure images of oscillating hips, not Whistler's mother
in her chair quieting an infant.

The ship is yet so far off that the flag's black background
suggests vultures hovering around human bones and skull
that the hyena eats guiltlessly since its closest relative

is the aardwolf. Without that motif, the flag
could be a nun's skirt spreading forgiveness as it moves with,
not against, the wind.

Hyenas have no need for religion unless its edible
and I don't need dead pirates who wash ashore
in the Bacardi bottles I can't get rid of, bad genies

who've inhabited the bottles long enough to evolve
into hyenas that laugh and whoop after the kill, after
they begin to feed.

They leave only tatters of black cloth
which could simply be the caribou's bloody
velvet that was supposed to fall off

or if the idea of forgiveness is correct
then the cloth is from a skirt
and being a nun didn't save me.

THOUGHTS ABOUT THE CARIBOU'S VELVET

You hate to look at it.
You hate to think of a rent dress
and the barbed wire it was ripped on
and the reasons behind the failed escape
and the failure
and the scratches that resemble
the markings on Ming dynasty treasures
and the blood rising to the tops of these wounds
as if something is ripening so fast
that you think of miracles.

You want to concentrate on the design itself, patterns
a fat happy lady in West Flanders puts in Chantilly
bobbin lace as she wraps threads around pegs and pins
stuck into pillows for the world's most beautiful voodoo.
You want to marvel that cruelty can be so artistic.

Against your will
the velvet stays on your mind, the strips hang
like rotting bandages. You catch yourself thinking you
wouldn't change them although the victim still bleeds.
The velvet hangs like enemy flesh from a bayonet
that fits your hand when you pick it up
although you killed no one.
You are never the same.
The blade resembles the thin victim too much.
Each branch of the antlers is another resemblance
as is your silence.
How does the caribou feel wearing these war memorials?
How do you feel, your ribs curved like the victim
and recoiling from your heart?

On the road from Barrington to Virginia Beach
you won't see any caribou, but the road itself
will seem like layers of hardened velvet
just before you collide with fences and telephone poles
having swerved to avoid that deer on your mind.

A RECONSIDERATION OF THE BLACKBIRD

Let's call him *Jim Crow.*

Let's call him *Nigger* and see if he rises
faster than when we say *abracadabra.*

Guess who's coming to dinner?
Score ten points if you said blackbird.
Score twenty points if you were more specific, as in the first line.

What do you find *from here to eternity?*
Blackbirds.

Who never sang for my father?
The blackbirds who came, one after the other, landed on the roof
and pressed it down, burying us alive.
Why didn't we jump out the windows? Didn't we have enough
    time?
We were outnumbered (13 on the clothesline, 4 & 20 in the pie).
We were holding hands and hugging like never before.
You could say the blackbirds did us a favor.

Let's not say that however. Instead let the crows speak.
Let them use their tongues or forfeit them.

Problem: What would we do with 13 little black tongues?

Solution: Give them away. Hold them for ransom. Make belts.
Little nooses for little necks.

Problem: The little nooses fit only fingers.

Solution: Get married.

Problem: No one's in love with the blackbirds.

Solution: Paint them white, call them visions, everyone will want
one.

THERE WILL BE ANIMALS

There will be animals to teach us
what we can't teach ourselves.

There will be a baboon who is neither stupid nor clumsy
as he paints his mandrill face for the war being waged
against his jungle.

There will be egrets in a few thousand years
who will have evolved without plumes so we cannot take them.

There will be ewes giving and giving their wool
compensating for what we lack in humility.

There will be macaws with short arched bills
that stay short because they talk without telling lies.

Mackerel will continue to appear near Cape Hatteras each spring
and swim north into Canadian waters so there can be continuity.

There will be penguins keeping alive Hollywood's golden era.

The chaparral cock will continue to outdistance man
twisting and turning on a path unconcerned with shortcuts.

Coffin fly dun will leave the Shawsheen River
heading for the lights of Lawrence. What they see in 48 hours
makes them adults who will fast for the rest of their short lives,
mating once during the next hour and understanding everything
as they drop into a communal grave three feet thick with family
reaching the same conclusions.

The coast horned lizard still won't be found
without a bag of tricks; it will inflate and the first
of six million Jewfish will emerge from its mouth.
We will all be richer.

John Dory will replace John Doe
so the nameless among us will have Peter's thumbmark on their
    cheek
and the coin the saint pulled from their mouths in their pockets.
Then once and for all we will know it is no illusion:
the lion lying with the lamb, the grandmother and Little Red
    Riding Hood
walking out of a wolf named Dachau.

TO ELIMINATE VAGUENESS

> *Instructions: substitute* irreversible damage *for* black
> *wherever it appears*

In the red-legged locust's black raids upon midwest soybeans,
in their illicit transmission of tapeworms and parasites
to quail, turkeys, and guinea fowl,
in all the black calendar days that are supposed
to indicate the ordinary.

In operating rooms body parts black with gangrene
are excised and trash cans seem to fill with dead crows.

There's a black crust two miles thick in Soweto, some on bread,
some around eyes, most on the streets where blood dried
into its own monument.

Then my mother's black face nothing can soften, the sweating,
the forgetting to sleep, the solidarity with anyone troubling,
the compassion only I knew she felt hugging a radio, singing
spirituals, sequestering herself in her widow's bedroom
praying for women unable to pray.

And what of Europeans, what of Asians and Latins who are
    irreversibly
damaged, whose gangrened minds should be excised but who are
    not black?

One day I noticed my mother had poured her face onto mine
and had given me the spirituals and lullabies.
I sang them when baskets of black clouds dumped
their transparent flowers over the convent

and the nuns' basic black didn't get wet
and they carted the flowers home in wheelbarrows
and arranged them like lullabies
and wept silently

as we were weeping, mother and daughter together
in my father's old rocker, the damage already done.

for Gary and the English 401 staff

PASSOVER POEM

God wipes his eyes.
God blinks as we do to resolve blur and disbelief.
He looks at the Jews he chose. They need a messiah.
He looks at my mother. Christ bought her with his blood.
Christ owns her. She is not free.
He looks at a million latino boys called *Jesús*. Jesus.
And recognizes not one of them as his son.
He looks at Asian eyes and tries to steady his hands.
The bomb didn't do it all.
He looks at blood smeared on Sharon Tate's doors and walls.
"Safe," he says, more umpire than God. Yet death does not pass
    over.
God blinks again. The earth is still there unchanged.
And poor God cannot pass the buck, he made the buck.

RUNNING OUT OF CHOICES

This is not about Beirut or El Salvador or Nicaragua,
words that get automatic respect
whether or not the speaker has anything to say.

I will not, therefore, mention Afghanistan, Poland
or Cambodia, not even the name of a favorite Chinese restaurant
for fear you might imagine the faces of Viet Cong peeping out
from the fried rice or little shipwrecked slant-eyed soldiers
floating toward shore on the tea bag in your cup.

I cannot even say Mississippi because someone might recall
that Medgar Evers was murdered there.

For related reasons I can't consider Alabama
unless I also mention churches and Easter dresses so ugly
bombs were thrown to eliminate the ugliness
while the girls were still in them.

Atlanta leads only to more bodies, some that didn't even
see puberty, never had sex, had never even been told about sex,
thought their own children would simply spring
from the split heads of cabbages on their mothers' counters
as their own split heads rot in gardens and dumps
making it possible to say that no burials are decent.

Go to New York and it's an abortion so old
I should have forgotten about it. Then a quick appraisal
of my child of ten who shoplifts and says very little
that isn't a lie and does nothing, including wash her face,
unless told. So now I wonder if maybe the wrong baby
was aborted. My love may be guilt,
no one's surprised,

not even that Marvin Gaye, Sr., has slain Marvin Gaye, Jr.
in *Los Ángeles,* city of mercy, city of angels.

I have no choice but to go home
to Cleveland, *Evergreen* cemetery, my father, Rebecca Robinson,
Sis. Winchell who killed her husband, Cordia Jackson, my pastor's
daughter, murdered in the projects, lye-based relaxer in
her short hair, other chemicals in the toilet; at her funeral
was the woman with whom Cordia's father, the pastor, had an
    affair
and also present, another preacher, father
of the young man who was my only temptation
during a marriage stronger now than ever
despite a kettle-black girl imported from Jamaica
who my husband found temporarily more exotic
than my blend of nigger and redskin;
back to my mother's picture window, bandaged with tape
where the bullet entered, only this time
it wasn't Kennedy's head

and now I'm in Texas, the lone star state,
but the state of loneliness is unbearable,
my star is an asterisk on the roster to emphasize
the minority presence, my star is in the constellation
Pisces, the fish, the symbol of Christians fed to lions;
fish is low in cholesterol, should be part of healthy diets,
I want long life, I want eternal life so I go to communion service,
I drink the blood, I eat the broken body
but the skimpy meal doesn't settle on my stomach, it rises
like Jesus.

Could this happen in Miami or
is that place too infested with foreigners like Haitians?
Everyone likes to say Haiti
because it gives hate a proper home.

And if a proper home is the idea
then it's back to Cleveland
where decent people walk with money in their hands or pockets
or purses or minds. The indecent give it away and are called
easy although to give is more blessed.

Sometimes I want to give reporters a piece of my mind,
not answers to ill-conceived, inconsiderate questions
but they might not give it back

and I'm selfish, I want everything that's mine,
the auction block, the war bonnet, Mr. T.'s wreath of chains,
the right to vote politicians out of office, the ashes
of crosses burnt on lawns to scatter like ugly rumors,
the black market because white markets don't sell mocha-colored
makeup except in summer when white people want tans
more than they don't want to be black.

Where can I go and mention Big Dan hoping to discuss
Daniel Boone's contributions to society and not a New Bedford
    gang rape?

Where can I go without somehow returning to Cleveland,
    Evergreen
cemetery, my father, Rebecca Robinson, Sis. Winchell who killed
her husband, Cordia Jackson, my pastor's daughter, murdered
in the projects I might have lived in had I not been so lucky.

GOOD AMNESIA

First of all, this was no accident.
I banged my head against the terminal walls
till I thought all the locomotives' whistles
were for me. Can you prove they weren't
or that I'm any worse off
for thinking I'm Catherine the Great
and look best in masculine clothes?
I deserve recognition
at least for never having been beautiful.
I shouldn't admit it but partitioning Poland
was easy for a woman. That there's one
in every household is no coincidence.
The rationing of food. The rationing.
People live off what we give them.
Some things I can't forget.

THE HARRIDAN

The harridan loses her temper all the time, claims drunk men
looking for a brothel took it; her diary

is full of lies. Two days later
she fishes her temper from the sewer where she lost it.

She grinds it with her teeth, the bitter taste
is sobering until her temper slips through the gaps,

comes out of salt & pepper shakers or the showerhead
and explodes over her like insecticide.

Such losses are minor,
her humpback is a cache. She can go for months

without an oasis, she has gone a whole life.
She does not know what to call this place

where butter clogs the pores of her bread
and suffocates it,

where geese fly backwards
closing their vee like a zipper,

where she has no way of knowing how long
before her upper and lower teeth lock

in her only marriage.

THE SEAMSTRESS

Where else could she find a lover so straight,
pure of form, so vertical, veering neither east nor west,
strictly an arctic, antarctic fellow?

The willful threads refuse to enter the eye
and she can't persuade them, not with her hands' seismic inability
to stay still long enough to pray for stillness.

So it doesn't stop, the planet keeps turning,
the galaxy doesn't halt its promiscuous travels
and the needle maintains verticality

not possessed by a single tree or opened arm cross,
stabs perversely and doesn't bend.
Only the seamstress changes,

the vinegar she's become cannot sterilize the needle
before it penetrates.
Tired, she examines the lengths of cloth,

the pieces, the separate lives,
the separate journeys, the proof
that stitching herself to the world doesn't work.

THE APOSTLE'S WIFE

Pubic hair greyed into cobwebs, a gift
of gimcrack fishing lines in a desert. The fraudulent sand
that isn't quick to let her enter.
Wormwood and anise come together as they used to
though restricted to dreams.
The absinthe formed mornings into bile.

The myriad closed eyes that merge and form her endless night
could be jarred like olives, exported for profit
were she not ashamed; she lost her husband
to another man, a regiment of giggling concubines
could be better understood. She is ordinary, sister
to the earthen water jug, crack for crack they are twins.
This Nazarene restores life to those who finally lose it.
Her only talent is being a woman who gets sick every month
because she can't turn her blood into wine.
Those who don't hear remain deaf to her existence.
Those who don't see keep waiting for the cloud to pass.

Her husband prefers the Nazarene,
perhaps only tired of being the head, of responsibility
his gender earned. Perhaps grateful to serve and obey,
perhaps always envious of his wife
and as ashamed of his envy as she of hers.

The Nazarene looks to her like a man.
Perhaps he is the light; she thinks it a foolish argument.
The eyes of night pursue the light thinking it knows
the way out, but the light is going where darkness has just been.
The stupid eyes aren't even tempted to open.

Night and day, shad rot at the ends of the lines on her palms.
This is what she caught. This is what belongs to her.
This is what she may keep. This is what remains of her fisherman
    husband.

Pine needles at the boundary of their thinness
are wider than a chance of return.

THE OWL IN DAYTIME

No one knows where the undertaker lives.
It should be impossible not to know.
In this village we find the owl in daytime
just to call him an ugly bird.
At night we have other habits
so we spill our guts to the owl,
tell him the worst tales we can think of,
how natural orifices evolved from wounds.
Yet the owl is too ugly to lose feathers.
Also, the owl has no neck.
Between the undertaker and the owl
there's no telling who's uglier.
Give us real differences,
not like night and day that embrace
like insecure lovers each time they meet.
Give us the undertaker's daughter,
the bread she makes.

THE UNDERTAKER'S DAUGHTER
MAKES BREAD

Even a frigid wife yields, even a stud has a soft spot.
He's with one of them now, forgiving
any man who deserts a totally paralyzed woman.
I don't forgive him
for making me believe in resurrections.
My belief is stronger than his or he'd work in a tent
and I'd be the faith healer's daughter,
myself cured.
Dough rises for me
no matter how I treat it, how I punch it.
Loaves line the counter like closed coffins.
Something I never want
is to wake from a long sleep
hungry.

THE UNDERTAKER'S DAUGHTER
FEELS NEGLECT

Tonight, a beautiful redhead
whose hair he's combed six times.
It is always the same. He never finds
his way to my room. My mother played dead
the night I was conceived.
Like him I'm attracted
to things that can't run away from me.
I spit-shine aluminum pans.

It's been years since the mailman came, years
since I woke in the middle of the night
thinking a party was going on downstairs,
thinking my father was a magician
and all those scantily clad women his assistants,
wondering why no one could hear me,
why I was made to disappear permanently in the box.
I seldom wake at all anymore.

MAI PEN RAI

I listen to the ragman's throaty drawl
as the curtains blow over me like mosquito netting.
His voice reminds me of chanting women doing laundry
with stones. Their hair falls over their eyes
like a curtain in shreds.
One of the Thai women pulls from the water a limb
washed down from Laos that doesn't match yesterday's.
She wears gifts from the ragman
who is now just below my window.
His stake-body truck moves as slow as a glacier.
The Thai woman can't move at all, the limbs are all around her,
a bone fence two feet high and growing.
At our family reunion we suck spareribs, purging them
of meat and marrow before we toss them.
They are not at all like boomerangs. The Thai woman
keeps these gifts too; it is warm inside the pyramid of bone.
I wish the ragman would wipe his forehead and unbutton
his shirt. I wish he wanted lemonade
and a date with the Thai woman.
Her arms can hold all the empty cradles in the Holy Land.
Her arms make whatever they contain holy.
A grenade in her arms is a bad egg
yet she sits on it and waves away observers, bids them run.
On behalf of stunted Bolivian Indians, shadows
pursued across the veldt and crippled one-legged crosses,
she lifts the sky saying *Mai pen rai, mai pen rai,*
it doesn't matter.
Perhaps I'd prefer mimosas, strawberries in season
and the view from Pike's Peak but not in this life;
everyday the ragman's drawl says *mai pen rai, mai pen rai*
and I believe.

> *Tanzan and Ekido were once traveling together*
> *down a muddy road. A heavy rain was still falling.*
> *Coming round a bend, they met a lovely girl in a silk*
> *kimono and sash, unable to cross the intersection.*
>
> *"Come on, girl," said Tanzan at once. Lifting her*
> *in his arms, he carried her over the mud.*
>
> *Ekido did not speak again until that night when*
> *they reached a lodging temple. Then he could no*
> *longer restrain himself. "We monks don't go near*
> *females," he told Tanzan, "especially not young and*
> *lovely ones. It is dangerous. Why did you do that?"*
>
> *"I left the girl there," said Tanzan. "Are you still*
> *carrying her?"*
>
> —*Zen parable*

This all happened in Ekido's first life
when he was tormented by any number of things,
the wax's pointless journey from the top of the candle
to the holder, the wick burning itself out without a fuss,
when at the top of a 300-foot Sitka spruce
he found another 300-foot Sitka spruce
and at the top of that one, another.
Some girls will never be able to stand on their bound feet.
Some girls will always have to be carried like straw
or a roll of carpet.
Monks especially, with their vow of silence, should know
what it's like not to be able to speak out
when you house a volcano.
This knowledge must be carried, remembered
first in its original smoky awareness
then as it gradually crystallizes
and the weight is felt, a woman is dancing her whole life
while the world dances on her toes.

TIMEX REMEMBERED

In the middle of an argument
I recall a high peak in the South Pacific,
a diver wearing only loin cloth and watch plunges,
surfaces, thrusts his watch towards the camera
and microphone; John Cameron Swazey takes over:
Timex, it takes a licking and keeps on ticking!

By fourth grade lickings were like bread crumbs,
too many to think about and irritating to the eyes.
I had seen Olivia jump from a window.
I had seen Dennis rape his sister's dolls
at her request.
I had seen a boy killed fifty yards from a hospital.
I remember telling the policeman who finally came
that the boy had dropped his bubblegum.
What would he do without the gum, without
a sweet taste forever on his tongue?
I was pushed aside. I retreated into silence, moved
through Glenville like a spirit. The pictures I took
hang even now in an internal gallery.
Morning Star Baptist Church was surely named
for something that didn't yet exist.

It didn't make sense when Tomasina's mother
whipped her up and down Durkee Avenue with a limb
from a peach tree. Tomasina had done what her mother did,
slept with a man, someone else's man.
Tomasina got a licking for her efforts,
her mother got Tomasina.
And yes, Tomasina kept on ticking,
the cross around her neck moved like a metronome
when she walked.

Then there was Blondell who stole
my piggy bank full of silver dollars
handed to my grandmother from her mother
who stole them from a white woman's pocketbook.
"She meant to pay me for services rendered," my great-
    grandmother said.
I said nothing when I saw Blondell again. Her gang stole forty
automobiles and dissected them. She knew no other science.
I listened to her popping Beechnut gum,
Blondell ticked like a bomb.

Louise thought her Navaho heart ticked too loudly
and I was so quiet she couldn't hear me above the racket
saying I liked her.
She returned to Piñon, Arizona in pieces
that each bore the signature of the craftsmen
who broke her with knives, bottle, and the tines
of forked tongues. *How* she said to me,
How I whispered but she didn't hear me,
she thought I said *This is how* and turned my back.
Nothing ticks between us.

The lickings haven't stopped.
Nowhere in the world have the lickings stopped.
What else translates as well as the sun
setting in a bloodbath?
Every heart bleeds just keeping us alive.
Oh the ticking, ticking. . . .
sometimes that's just Old Lady Samodale
trying to grow flowers, not even thinking
about race, not even worrying about who's winning
the human race, just doing her spring cleaning, making room
in her mind for flowers.
Rowdy youth ride by after a riot and tell her
this neighborhood is a ghetto now. They uproot her flowers
and trample them or try to smoke them.

Their Afros remind her of barbed wire.
She knows more about ghettos than they ever will.
Her daffodils were yellow as crayons.
Sometimes the ticking is Mrs. Samodale sinking
to her knees, shaking her head, going *tch, tch, tch*
a long way from Czechoslovakia. There's no freedom
anywhere, no freedom from the *Timex* watch, the accuracy
of its score.

LANDSCAPE WITH SAXOPHONIST

The usual is there,
nondescript trees opened like umbrellas,
pessimists always expecting rain,
chickadees whose folding and unfolding wings
suggest the shuffling and reshuffling
of the cardsharp's deck;
nothing noteworthy except the beginning saxophonist
blowing with the efficacy of wolves addicted to pigs,
blowing down those poorly built houses,
the leaves off the trees, the water in
another direction, the ace of spades
into the ground with the cardsharp's bad intentions.
The discord and stridency set off landslides
and avalanches; his playing moves the earth
not lovers who are satisfied too quickly
and by the wrong things.

DRAFTY CORNER IN A TOW-AWAY ZONE

Aerial views of Kilauea's lava flow suggest a smile,
crooked as if the hand carving it was unsure or in a hurry,
danger defied for the sake of a smile.
We always smile for the camera
even when wolves pile up like leaves around our doorsteps.
No matter where I went, in the midst of epidemic or typhoon
I took pictures; a man balancing his life on a last dime
is in a dusty portfolio on my desk. Sometimes it's good
to think of: *fromage, queso, ost, käse, cheese,* to smile
and forget everything else.
What about the man balancing his life on five millimeters
who can't fit a smile on his narrow province?
There's also the woman living in the shadow of
a downtown office building who smiles at a nearby lamppost
and puts her arms around it in an intimate slowdance,
her hips barely moving, timed to the lamppost's movement.
I don't know the circumstances that brought her to
this drafty corner in a tow-away zone,
I don't know if she survived all her children
in a suspicious house fire
or whether this mistress had to grow old alone most of the time.
I don't know whether her hair was lost to disease or frustration
and idle fingers. I cannot smile at her decision to love
a lamppost, man-made, twice removed from God.
I cannot smile at her lack of disappointment when the lamppost
ignores her. I cannot smile at her anticipation of neglect.
I cannot smile at her image of herself that puts her
the same distance from God as the lamppost.
The camera pointed at her like a thick inhuman finger won't even
venture into her field of vision, it hides behind telephoto and ferns.
She says *cheese* because she doesn't have any,
she still says *cheese* after the photographer has gone,
after she is made famous on the news.

POSSIBILITIES THAT REQUIRE TOMBSTONES

I go there often,
slabs of grey marble and red granite
are heavy and enormous place cards
for guests who arrive by air.

The day to be there is when legions
of parachutes descend
as if fatigued birds grabbed onto clouds.
Like sheets the chutes land
on beds green with sandbur, teosinthe.

Every grave grows its own flowers, yellow
as the sun in a child's drawing
as a girl's hair in the same drawing, a yellow
that exists only in a box of Crayolas
and in the child's happiness and logic.

Some tombstones date back a century
or more. In a hundred years
roots of what was planted have probably
found China where birds bug at them for hours
as if worms. I can see puzzled farmers
fleeing fields where dozens of fatigued birds
fainted after giving all to the struggle.
I can see farmers returning stealthily, singly,
tugging at the same roots, pulling our fathers
and mothers as if rescuing those tossed overboard.
I can see them pulling and pulling with strength
not normally needed, pulling without knowing what
they pull nor caring; fishers of men, any man.
Sons take over when their fathers' beards grow so long
the pulling of beard is confused with root.

It is the missing magic;
the magician could enthrall us forever
if the scarf were long enough.

FISHER STREET

I like to walk down Fisher Street
Everybody hangs laundry in the backyard

most of it white and durable

I think of hundreds of gallons of bleach
zinc tubs, clothes stirred with sticks

Fels Naptha, water hot enough to dissolve skin

mortuary stillness forced on children during a sermon
the clerical collar stiff and sturdy as a blade

a rude white, too much contrast with his face. I look away

think of monks mashing grapes
staining their feet the blue-black of a man from Niger

I think they'll never get their feet clean

Chix diapers white as glory, so clean
they're cut into placemats or made into pillows

once the children are grown.

I think of graduation, colorless, odorless diamonds
yellow, white, and black gold

I think of weddings, bachelors, spinsters, gigolos and hookers

I think of degrees, murder, justifiable homicide
the dead man's clothes hanging dry

pants pockets pulled out and exposed

shirts buttoned to the throat, sleeves at the wrist
all faded, white after so many washings. The widow's hair

Everything plain as day.

I want everybody listening to the same 24-hour station
everybody singing along till hoarse voices

make only whispers and prayers

Sing till it's cold out and the song rises like vapor,
the seen breath of winter, white and bleached

like all that laundry waving on the line, dancing to the song

struggling like all of us to be free.
I don't expect to see

any other angels.

THE ROAD TO TODOS SANTOS IS CLOSED

That's a movie about events that don't happen where I live.
That's a documentary about a village you can't visit.

Remember not to ask how the black river was named
if you don't want to know what happens to blood
after the ground has been saturated.

A song comes from a rooftop pointed like a beak
and the beak is wired shut but the song gets out
and the song says the road is closed
and the song says this is not where Dorothy went
and the song says this is not what the dove saw
after the waters subsided
and the song says what *todos santos* means.

Todos santos means all that refers to God
Todos santos means all saints
Todos santos means lives of unquestionable repute
Todos santos means everything holy
          not just the seven days from Palm Sunday to Easter
          not just the magdalens and madonnas.
And the song is for those who speak English and need help
understanding exactly where it is that we can't go.

The road to Todos Santos is closed.
You can't even bribe the guards.
You can't even get them drunk to seduce them.
They are drunk. They've been seduced.
That's why they won't open the road.
Their skin is so hard you can't even shoot them.

There's an extra syllable Emilio
gives English words beginning with "s."
I wish to be as sure we'll get back what's missing.
I wish to have similar faith that Todos Santos can be accessed
without a road.

DOUBTS DURING CATASTROPHE

*The hand of the Lord was upon me, and set me down
in the midst of the valley; it was full of bones.*

—*Ezekiel 37:1*

Being in God's hand doesn't mean being in a full house.
It means Mother Hubbard being a grave robber
cloaking herself in hood and cape dark as her act.
This is what one does when one has dogs to beware of:
dig up the prize begonias, a femur, fibula, a tibia, phalanges.
She didn't even love these bones when they walked the earth
in her man.

All it takes is faith
the size of a mustard seed that makes a real princess
toss and turn all night though it's under thirty mattresses.
I've never felt the wedding cake beneath my pillow,
the hard slice is now an artifact archaeologists attach
to a Jurassic Behemoth.

No better time to recall God's fascination
with his image. He put something of himself
in every creation. When he was tired
he made lazy idiots. When he had hiccups
he made tumbleweeds. When he needed a twin
he made Adam. And whenever he needed to
he watched Adam seduce Eve. And when once Eve refused
God's eyebrows raised, merged and flew off, a caracara
seeking carrion. And then there was wrath. *Vengeance
is mine* he said. And then there was his seduction
of Mary who had to submit, could not disobey the Lord.

If he told her he had not created disobedience
he lied.

Now the cyclone spirals above my house; I vow not to go to
    heaven
if that's the only ladder.

Thylias Moss received a B.A. from Oberlin College and an M.A. from the University of New Hampshire. She currently teaches at Phillips Academy, Andover, Massachusetts. Moss is the recipient of a 1987 Artist's Fellowship from the Massachusetts Arts Council. She has published poems in *Callaloo, Obsidian II, Indiana Review,* and other journals. She has also published *Hosiery Seams on a Bowlegged Woman,* a collection of poems.